A SHARED LAND

A One State
One Government
Peace Plan

TARA ARONSON

A SHARED LAND

AT SOME POINT, possibly very soon, the people of Israel will realize that it is impossible to achieve safety through a military victory because a structure which would constitute such a victory simply does not exist. At that point the door for peace opens, and it is essential to have a realistic peace plan on the table.

Currently there are three main peace plans being considered: a two-state plan, a confederation, and a one-person one-vote democracy. The first two plans would be asking a Palestinian government to deal with the settlers—an almost impossible situation. Additionally, a two-state solution does not include the right to return for Palestinians—factor of great importance. The third plan, a one person one vote democracy, is feared by both groups for the possibility that one group might dominate the other. I have conceptualized a peace plan which, while possibly the most difficult to implement, I believe would have the highest chance of long-term success.

Before going on to describing my vision, I would like to suggest that we reframe the conflict from being one between Palestinians and Israelis to one between those who are striving for peace and those who are striving for war. The war mongers justify their own atrocities with the atrocities committed by the other side. They use hate and the concept of a shared enemy to keep themselves in power.

Those striving for peace do the opposite: The Alliance for Middle East Peace is a coalition of over 160 organizations, with hundreds of thousands of Palestinians and Israelis striving to building cooperation and peace among their communities. Awad Darawshe was a Palestinian Israeli medic who, on October 7th, sacrificed his own life, trying to save lives of the injured at the Tribe of Nova music festival. Jewish Israeli peace activists are using their own bodies (and cameras) to create a protective presence, trying to shield Palestinian farmers from settler violence.

What is needed is a structure which shifts power in the direction of those striving for peace. I believe that a joint government with power carefully balanced would accomplish this in a way that trying to balance power between two opposite governments would not, and cannot.

I am envisioning a single state with a government in which

the power of different groups would be carefully balanced, and usually intertwined. Many positions usually filled by one person would be filled by a team of one Palestinian, one Jew, and sometimes a third person who is either neither, or both. This would include the head of state, teachers, judges, juries, prison guards, and police. These teams would be formed voluntarily by the participants before running for office or applying for a job. This is the factor that would switch power to those Israelis and Palestinians who are able to work with a partner from the other side. The model of this team approach is already in use in Hand in Hand Schools where classes are bilingual and taught by a team of one Palestinian teacher, and one Jewish teacher. They have developed training programs to give their teachers the skills needed to operate in mixed cultural teams. Now they are also training staff in schools that are mixed due to geography, rather than choice, and these training programs are going well. This is a good indicator of the potential of some who are not currently seeking intercultural relationships to be able to function in them.

Certainly, there would be some, perhaps many, who are currently employed, in any of the above positions mentioned above who, even with training, would not be able to adjust to working as part of a mixed cultural team. It is important that this be provided for, and these people be given support and assistance in making a career change.

The country's decision-making body might also be formed by teams, or might be formed and balanced by a different design. Also needing to be examined is the question of decision making by majority vote, as is done in most western democracies, or by consensus, as is more usual in villages. I suggest something in-between. This means that the decision-making process would be slower than in a rule by majority situation, and this in turn means that as much as possible, the details of the government should be worked out before the new government is adopted.

In conceptualizing the details of design for the country I am trying to take into account that virtually everyone in the country has been traumatized, some by being victims of atrocities, some by committing atrocities, some by both, and virtually everyone by fear. Virtually everyone has been exposed to hate propaganda, whether they endorse it or not. Many have head injuries which affect the ability to function in ways that may be a mixture of obvious and elusive. Many have physical injuries which are serious and permanent. In developing my plan, I am constantly asking two questions: What structures help deal with the situation just described? What structures help any country to function better?

1. An unusual approach to creating a jury: This approach would also make use of the team concept. Instead of randomly selecting a temporary untrained group to make incredibly important decisions, teams of jurists would be elected. As with the head of the country, a team would either consist of one Palestinian and one Jew, or this with the addition of one person who is neither or both. Each jury would be made up of seven teams, each team getting one vote. Once elected, jurists would go through some training, probably a few weeks full time. They would then work full time as jurists for a term. When the term ends, jurists could run for re-election. There would be no limit on how many times they could run for re-election. If a person who was neither a Palestine nor a Jew was being tried, he or she could request a jury with teams of three, rather than two, increasing the chances of there being some jurors of their own ethnicity, or at least increasing the different perspectives available to the jury. Since there would initially be a great need to examine, one by one, the situation of prisoners, and free those who, in the context of the new government, would not be a danger to society, there would initially be a great need for jurists. Given that this need should reduce over time, the jurists need to have alternative work that can be done on a flexible schedule. In this way a shortage of jurists would be prevented, and anyone awaiting trial, could be assured that the wait will not be long. Facing the unknown is a pain that can be minimized.

2. The right of return would be guaranteed to all Palestinians and Jews, to the degree possible. Since this would increase the population density in many places, it might necessitate mixing agriculture with manufacturing, something which is already happening on many kibbutzim. This could also happen in rebuilt Palestinian villages. Exactly where the rebuilt Palestinian villages would be, and where the kibbutzim would be, is a multifaceted question.

When I began writing this document, I was thinking that the injustice that many Palestinian villages were raized and replaced by kibbutzim simply cannot be redressed. However, now I am thinking that it might be possible, to at least some extent. I believe that the number of Palestinians for whom it is very important to return to the specific piece of land their family had lived on for centuries is much greater than the number of kibbutzniks for whom a specific piece of land is important. I believe that what is important for kibbutzniks is to remain living and working with each other. If a sufficient financial incentive was offered there might be many kibbutzim that would not mind relocating. My overall thought is that nobody should be forced to move from where they currently live, but financial incentives can be offered for doing so. This does mean that there are wrongs that will not be redressed. My hope is that efforts to get as close as possible to this goal will still bring the peace.

I am certain that there is a concern that putting a rebuilt Palestinian village right next to a kibbutz would be an invitation for violence. My response is that there is no inherent enmity between Palestinians and Jews, rather the enmity developed over land ownership. With both groups owning their own land the fuel that feeds the enmity is gone. The chances of violence could further be reduced by having the children of both communities attending the same Hand in Hand school, and the parents regularly meeting together.

It also needs to be noted that granting Palestinians and Jews the right to return, but not everyone else, is discrimination on the basis of ethnicity. I see no solution here as no country could take in all the refugees in the world. I do recommend that there be a department of the government whose main job is to work with other countries, and with international agencies to improve the situation of refugees, as well as to address the causes of there being so many refugees.

3. Torture would be both forbidden, and defined in great detail. Without an explicitly detailed definition of torture, it is impossible to enforce laws against its use. Public education as to why torture is wrong must be ongoing. One would think that this is something human beings would not forget. History repeatedly proves otherwise.

4. The measures used for societal well-being would be carefully chosen. I find it astonishing that the Gross National Product is commonly regarded as a gold standard measure of economic well-being. The GNP measures production but not loss, destruction, distribution, or environmental damage. I would advocate using the following measures: a low rate of crime, a low rate of incarceration, the absence of anyone being without food, shelter, or medical care, and a steady decrease in environmental destruction, reaching zero as soon as possible. In striving to achieve these goals I recommend making full use of the research of Dr. Bruce Boghosian, proving mathematically that in a free enterprise system, unless wealth difference is kept within reasonable boundaries, through the use of taxes and transfers, it will expand indefinitely. Eventually it will turn any democracy into an oligarchy, even in the presence of elections. This is a mathematical phenomena that will happen even in the absence of greed. However, human nature being what it is, once wealth difference expands beyond reasonable boundaries, greed does enter the picture, causing the process to accelerate. The manner of the interface of this mathematical phenomena and human greed is the reason why, in order for the redistribution to be of sufficient quantity it must be through a combination of taxes and voluntary charity, not voluntary charity alone.

5. Truth and Reconciliation: These are two extremely complex topics. Following are my thoughts—not set in stone. The implementation of the Shared Land Peace Plan ultimately depends on the agreement of both parties. Were the plan to include incarceration of those who committed atrocities it would never be accepted. The atrocities are simply too great in number. It is as if mass insanity has taken over the land and cruelty has become a mandated drug. Meir Baruchin, an Israeli schoolteacher, was arrested, interrogated for hours, and put in solitary confinement for expressing on Facebook his opinion that the mass bombing of Gaza is not justified by the atrocities of October 7th. Israeli human rights groups find themselves unable to reduce the use of torture in prisons.

However, hope lies in the fact that an increasing number of people want to end the war simply to be free of violence, and to not sacrifice their children and grandchildren. The news outlet, Haaretz, estimates that approximately fifty percent of Israelis are now in this category. This could open the door for the creation of a governmental structure capable of preventing the continuation of atrocities. This is the goal that should not be sacrificed.

However, it is reasonable that someone who has held a position of power and used it to abuse those over whom he or she had control, should not be allowed to again hold a position of power. This is a part of insuring that the atrocities do not continue.

Along with the cessation of atrocities, there is a need for healing. For many there is healing in participating in a forum in which people can speak about atrocities they endured, and/or those they committed. In such a forum, allowing arts of every kind to be used as a means for communication can enhance the healing process. As people heal, the country heals.

There is no perfectly fair way to address restitution. Shepherds lost access to public pastures which they had never owned, but upon which their livelihoods depended. Farmers lost orchards which they had planted, and in which they knew every tree as an individual. Yet they may have rented rather than owned the land. However, it is possible to get close to the goal of being fair by having a very high level of tax-based redistribution. Land grants and start up business grants, based on need, should be readily available. In addition, as will be elaborated upon later, there needs to be a minimum income which assures everyone food and shelter. This creates a strong country without poverty and without massive amounts of wealth and power being collected into the hands of a few.

6. Will Some Remain Committed to Violence? I believe the plan I am describing would vastly reduce violence for the simple reason that most people are receiving what they want. However, there would probably remain some who cling to the goal of annihilating the other side. Religious scholars who oppose fanaticism and violence might be able to play a role here. What is certain is that a government comprised of Jewish-Palestinian teams would be in a far better position to deal with extremists on both sides than a government that was primarily one group or the other.

7. Building Community and Creating Structures that Leave No One Out: This is a subject that is as complex as it is important. My goal here is to address factors which I feel are most critical. First of all, everybody needs to be assured, without the need for vast paperwork, of food, shelter, medical care, and a means of gathering with other people. The usual objection to this is that it would create laziness. My answer is that this is not true if the structure is such that there is an advantage to working. I am not suggesting equal income for everyone, I am suggesting a minimum income. It may be that the best structure for accomplishing this is to provide everyone with a very basic income that could cover necessities. Salaries, pensions, disability payments etc. would be planned to be in addition to this income.

In putting this whole picture together, it is also important to realize that there are many medical conditions which may be disabling before they progress enough to be diagnosed, or even proven to exist. There are also many rare diseases which likewise can be difficult to diagnose or prove to exist. There is no perfectly fair way to deal with this. However, providing everyone with at least a basic income that provides food, shelter, and medical care, is light years away from leaving someone in a state of absolute desperation, with no access to necessities. Some may say this is too expensive. My answer is that if desperation turns someone to crime this is far more difficult and costly to deal with than providing everyone with necessities. The subtleties here are extremely important. In the city where I used to work, there is a homeless shelter that goes to great lengths to make guests feel welcome. The shelter helps with job training, counseling , finding medical care—whatever is needed. The sense of caring emanating from this showed up one day at the clinic where I worked with small children. I commented to my aide how impressed I was that one of our two-year-olds had spent the whole morning hosting a new child, making sure he was comfortable and happy. My aide replied, "Well, they were together for a month at the shelter, so he feels responsible for him, like a brother." I believe the institutions created by Sattar Edhi in Pakistan are usually successful in this and should be studied. He makes great use of the principle that people with one kind of need can help people with other kinds of needs.

Another factor that is critical in creating a sense of community is simply having places where people can gather. I believe there are apartment buildings in Nordic countries which include a kitchen and dining room large enough to serve all the residents. Residents take turns cooking meals for all who want to come. Even apartment buildings which do not have this, need to have some place where people can gather. Homes need to be built with the understanding that they are homes, not barracks. Part of this ties in with controlling wealth difference, which is essential for enabling sufficient funding for public works. Part of this lies in understanding the importance of beauty, of skilled architecture and of careful design.

8. Education: This section is longer and goes into more detail than you might expect. The reason is that all of these details are relevant to the goal of reducing anger, violence, and aggression while increasing the development of positive interests and the ability to work with others in a way that leaves no one out. Let's begin by building upon the models that have already been created, the Hand in Hand schools already described, and Mar Elias Educational Institute, founded by the Palestinian Melkite priest, Father Elias Chacour. Both are intercultural and bilingual (trilingual by high school.) Father Chacour tells his students "God does not kill. All are born as babies created in the image and likeness of God. Christians, Muslims, and Jews are blood brothers, children of Abraham. Peace with justice is the dream and the right of all human beings." Mar Elias Educational Institute has three thousand students ranging from preschoolers to university students. In some ways, both Mar Elias Educational Institute and the Hand in Hand schools are microcosms of the one state vision about which I am writing.

I also suggest studying the educational system of Finland. Finland is a country with a high rate of redistribution through taxes and transfers, and a correspondingly low rate of crime and incarceration. They have little or no hunger or unsheltered homelessness. I believe this attitude of inclusion is what has enabled Finland to do away with standardized testing, seeing it as an obstacle to co-operative, developmentally appropriate learning. Not until children are old enough for career training, usually about age fifteen, are they expected to deal with the pressures of taking tests. The tests taken are related to the career and academic choices being made by the student. For all ages the curriculum is designed to make full use of three-dimensional learning, using, rather than suppressing movement, and providing learning through manipulatives. Teachers are rigorously trained, and then given trust and freedom.

To this I add my own perspective that periodic screenings by speech therapists, occupational therapists, and physical therapists could accomplish what is hoped to be accomplished by standardized testing. Following is my reasoning: a standardized test can identify that a certain six-year-old is delayed in reading. Therapeutic screenings can identify that the child lacks the ability to co-ordinate the left and right side of his or her body, which prevents the proper development of visual perception, which causes difficulty in learning to read. Therapeutic screenings, and when needed, evaluation and treatment, can prevent all kinds of problems, ranging from behavior problems to an increased probability of joint injury. The benefits of these screenings are not limited to school age children. These screenings should begin in infancy and continue through life, in the same manner as dental checkups.

Returning to the topic of educating children, I would like to add another element which I believe is important in any educational system, but particularly critical in a situation where virtually all the children have been traumatized. Children who are aggressive need comprehensive treatment. This might include providing such children with smaller classes, a specially trained teacher, and when needed, a one-on-one aid whose role is to be a mentor, friend, and sometimes also a playmate. This situation can be completely transforming. Here, I would like to tell a story, from my work in a pediatric clinic which illustrates this.

One morning, I heard a newly arrived two-year-old shouting "Shut up!" to a five-year-old who had been with us for a year. The five-year-old responded by smiling at the younger one, putting his hand gently on the little one's wrist and saying, "Don't say that. Speak nice. Do you want to play catch?" He spent the next hour mentoring the little one on the game of catch. A year earlier, this five-year-old had been one of the most aggressive children we had ever treated. For the first two months he was with us, his one-on-one aide made sure that he was never within kicking distance of another child. Gradually, he learned play skills, first with his aide, and then with other children. His need for a one-on-one aide began to decrease, and eventually ended. Now, a year later, he demonstrated that he had absorbed the value that someone who isn't nice needs a teacher, mentor, friend to teach them how to be so.

It is critically important that the staff working with these children have a natural inclination and love of doing so. It would be better to hire someone with less training, and give more on the job training, than place a teacher who is not comfortable with this situation in this role. This is not a criticism of such a teacher. Different teachers have different strengths. The goal is to create structures which leave no one out, neither teachers, nor students.

I would like to go into some additional detail about working with these children, because I have experience in this area, which gives me some not widely known knowledge. Emotionally fragile children tend to feel more secure when objects fit securely into specific places. For instance, a geometric puzzle works better than a bowl of shapes with pattern cards. Matching cards work better if they are hung on hooks or slide into a frame, than if they are simply placed together on an open surface. Symbolic toy animals often work better than accurate replicas, especially if the animals are scary ones. Objects that roll or slide or drop through a hole and go "clink," increase interest. Long, thin, brightly colored objects sitting loose on a shelf (Montessori number rods), tend to invite misbehavior. When I was teaching a class with many fragile children, I replaced these with shorter, thicker, wood colored counting rods which fit securely into a rectangular frame. Four sets of these framed rods can be built into a tower, which, until the moment of writing this, I have always regarded as being able to make a wonderfully exciting, yet safe implosion.

As I write this, I realize that I have never worked with children who have been bombed, for whom such an implosion of blocks might be frightening. How best to work with children who have been in war, and also, sometimes in prison, needs to be discussed by those with experience and knowledge in this area.

For some children, even the level of extra support I have described above will not be enough. This is especially true since there will be many children with head injuries. In these cases, I recommend using the Son-Rise program developed by the Option Institute. In this program the teacher, mentor, friend works with the child one on one in a room where there is nothing the child could do that would be dangerous and have to be stopped. I once spoke to a mother who, partnering with her husband, used this program with their six-year-old daughter who had no communication skills, not even gesturing or eye contact, no awareness of personal hygiene, and was dangerously violent. The doctor told the parents they had no choice but institutionalization. Instead, they chose this program which immediately provided the safety that was needed while leaving the door of hope open. One of the parents worked with the child all her waking hours. Five years later, their daughter was delightfully social, still cognitively delayed, but able to speak in three-to-five-word sentences. Few parents would have the stamina to do what this family did, but a school system could do it, if the larger society understood the need, and was willing to fund the program. (In this situation, of the program being operated by a public institution, for the safety of both the child and the staff member, I would consider security cameras essential.) Some might say that such a program is simply too expensive. My answer is that a lifetime of institutionalization, be it in prison or a mental hospital, is far more expensive. Some might wonder how a program like this could help if there is physical brain damage. The answer is that other parts of the brain take over.

Teenagers feel more secure if they are involved in career training. This doesn't mean the choice of career is set for life, but one foot is being put down in the land of adulthood. It is also important that teenagers study child development, and be given hands an experience working with children, in a well supervised environment. The importance of this is expressed in two quotes from teenage aides who worked with me in a pediatric rehabilitation agency.

"I never knew how much fun children can be, and I never knew how much work it takes. Now I know that I definitely want to have children someday, and I know I want to wait until I am really ready."

"I used to think life was a choice between being good or being happy. Now I know it can be both."

An additional way to leave no one out would be offering sign language as an elective. If many hearing people knew sign language this would vastly improve the lives of deaf people. An additional reason for teaching sign language is that it uses both sides of the brain, increases spatial awareness, cognitive flexibility, and critical thinking.

9. Is the concept of the peace plan, A Shared Land, realistic?
I am quite certain that many who read this document would say

that the concept is nice, but completely unrealistic—impossible. For this reason, I would like to describe several events which seemed completely impossible—and yet happened.

During the holocaust, the French village of Le Chambon rescued a number of Jews roughly equal to the number of their own population, most of whom were pacifists. The village was located about twenty minutes from the Nazi headquarters, and the Nazis were fully aware of what they were doing. There is no earthly explanation as to why the village was not raized, as were so many other villages. It was as if a force of goodness was protecting the village—a force beyond human comprehension.

When my Montessori teacher, Lakshmi Kripalani, found herself a refugee in a refugee camp, she saw a great need for a school. With the only resources available being sticks, stones, grass, flowers, ground, the helping hands of fellow refugees, and the fact that some of the refugees had knowledge they could teach, a fully functioning school was created.

Sattar Edhi, a street vendor with an eight-grade education, and great vision, facilitated the creation of schools, hospitals, ambulances, soup kitchens, job training centers, orphanages, and institutions based on the principle of mutual assistance, caring for those with every kind of special need.

Nicholas Winton was a British man who rescued 669 Jewish Czechoslovakian children from the holocaust. He began by saying, "If something is not completely impossible, then by definition it is possible." Let us adopt this attitude.

10. The goal of the original Zionists was to create a country in which Jews could always find refuge and safety. The problem with the plan for doing so was that it included an unjust removal of an indigenous population. I believe the plan outlined here is a more realistic one for providing both Jews and Palestinians with safety and security.

A CONDENSED HISTORY

—AND—

Description of the Current Situation
Presented Through an Annotated Bibliography

Blood Brothers by Elias Chacour, with David Hazard—The earliest part of Elias's childhood was almost paradisical, feeling safe and secure in a traditional tightly knit Palestinian village, called Biram. The first crack in his little heaven came when his father told the family that across the ocean was a Satan of a man called Hitler, who killed Jews simply because they were Jews. "I was not prepared for such horrifying words. Someone killing Jews. The thought chilled me. Made my stomach uneasy." (pg. 28) Soon after this, Elias began to experience the Nakba (expulsion of Palestinians). Soldiers told all the villagers they needed to leave—but only for two weeks. They were never allowed to return. After they found shelter in the village of Gish, soldiers again came. This time they came with trucks and loaded up all the men and older boys, and drove them away. Only about half were eventually able to make their way home. Struggling to understand what was happening Elias poured out his heart to the one friend he knew would always be with him, no matter what the circumstances—Jesus of Nazareth.

The writing style of this book makes it very user friendly for the American public. It's a hard-to-put-down, human interest story. Additionally, should the reader wish more information, it is readily available. The story of Biram is well known, available on-line, and with little controversy as to what happened. I urge anyone who reads this book and agrees with me, to promote it in any way possible. I believe that if this were a well-read book in the United States, our country's ability to make informed decisions about our Middle East policies would be significantly improved.

+ + +

The Lemon Tree by Sandy Tolan—When Bashir Khairi was six years old his father moved the family from the beautiful home he had built in al- Ramla to a one room house in Ramallah, and then to a one room house in Gaza, both moves for the purpose of seeking safety. Jewish refugees with an infant daughter named Dalia moved into the Khairi house. As Dalia grew up, she began to wonder why the Arabs who built the beautiful house she lived in had left. When she was nineteen the opportunity for her to find out opened. Three shy young Arab men were standing at her door asking if they might come in to see the house that one of them had once lived in. Thus began a relationship that lasted their entire lives, not always a smooth one, but a deep one. More than fifty years later Dalia said, "It is deeper than friendship. It has to do with family." Bashir said he wished there was a forest of Dalias.

Sandy Tolan is incredibly thorough in his documentation. He spares no effort in research. Whenever he finds contradiction, he reports both sides. While he strives to write history as if it were a novel, this does not in any way reduce the incredible volume of the history he relates.

✦　✦　✦

Children of the Stone by Sandy Tolan—This book beautifully carries the message that it is possible to fight a non-violent fight by teaching children to work, and practice, and make beautiful, powerful music, and use the power of that music to speak against injustice, and advocate for justice. Again, Sandy Tolan's writing is incredibly filled with documentation.

✦　✦　✦

The Jews' State (of) Theodor Herzl by Henk Overberg—to clarify—this book, written by Henk Overberg, is a translation and commentary of Herzl's book. Overberg's goal is to enable a modern reader to understand Herzl in the context of the world in which he was living. Thus a significant portion of the book is devoted to describing European thought in the nineteenth and early twentieth century. A belief in the superiority of intellectual European culture over other cultures, and a belief that being dominant was the best method of protecting oneself from oppression, were both prevalent. Herzl's plans for the indigenous population are presented on page ninety-one, "We must expropriate gently the private property on the estates assigned to us." (purchase land and evict tenants) "We shall try to spirit the penniless population across the border by procuring employment for it in transit countries, while denying it any employment in our own country." (the penniless meaning those who were evicted from their rented farms and orchards) "Both the process of expropriation and the removal of the poor must be carried out discreetly and circumspectly." My own perception is that while Herzl's words "must be carried out discreetly and circumspectly," make it clear that he knew what he was proposing was morally wrong, he had no comprehension of the magnitude of the atrocity he was suggesting. Overberg makes it clear that at other times Herzl proposed alternate approaches. Unfortunately, the reality today makes it clear that this did not reduce the effect of his original words. What played out is that European Jews offered landlords unusually high prices to buy their land. Once the land was purchased tenants were evicted. To the European perception purchasing land with the intention of evicting all the tenants was legal and fair. To the Middle East perception this was an act of agression to be avenged. Thus, began more than a century of violence, with each side absolutely certain that the other was the initial aggressor. Tragically, the belief today remains prevalent that if life is made sufficiently untenable for Palestinians, they will disappear. Likewise the belief remains prevalent that this needs to be done in a way that is not obvious, or even could be disguised all together.

Overberg's intention seems to be that of presenting information as comprehensively and accurately as possible without expressing an opinion of his own. Yet in some way, simply by his efforts in the direction of accuracy and thoroughness, he expresses an opinion that opposes glorification and oversimplification.

❖ ❖ ❖

Plowshares into Swords by Arno J. Mayer—While Arno Mayer puts the same incredible effort into comprehensiveness and accuracy as Henk Overberg, Mayer's intention is definitely to express an opinion in support of those early Zionists whose goal was a binational state in which Jews were neither the majority, nor dominant—Ahad Haam, Martin Buber, Judah Magnes, Chaim Nachman Bialik, Yitzhak Epstein, Henrieta Szold, and others. There were also organizations promoting this goal, Brit Shalom and Ihud among them. The goal would not be to attract as many Jews as possible, but to create a center for the development of Jewish thought.

For four hundred pages, Mayer documents the political struggles in great detail. On the last page he quotes Moria Shlomot, director of Peace Now, saying, "The day will come when we have to explain to our children why the State of Israel starved a whole civilian population and how the army of a people who had experienced ghettoes cut off entire villages with ditches and barbed wire. Any rational person understands that this will not bring security. Determined terrorists cross any obstacle, but the despair caused by poverty and starvation will push more and more people into the arms of Islamic fundamentalists."

✦ ✦ ✦

The Rabin Memoirs by Yitzhak Rabin and ***The General's Son*** by Miko Peled—I believe I can best describe these books in relationship to each other. Much of Miko Peled's book is about his father, Matti Peled. On page sixty-nine Miko writes about his father and Rabin, "For thirty years they had fought side by side and worked together to build the Israeli army, and in 1967 led it to the final conquest of the 'Promised Land.'" However, they then began to diverge. Where Rabin saw a Palestinian problem, Matti saw Palestinians with whom he wanted to be able to communicate. He learned not only the language of Arabic, but also its literature and poetry, and developed many close friendships with Arabs of varying nationalities. Initially Matti Peled fully supported the Oslo Accords, but eventually he began wondering why the settlements were allowed to keep expanding, and why Israel was ignoring good faith deadlines. He finally came to the conclusion that Rabin did not want a peace that was based on a fully independent Palestinian state. On August 16, 1993 Matti Peled stated this publicly, permanently severing his relationship of friendship with Rabin. Matti also felt that, "Arafat, who had put everything on the line for peace, was being treated with contempt."

Yet, Rabin, in 1976 had stated, "I see in Gush Emunim [the settlement movement,] one of the most acute dangers in the whole phenomenon of the State of Israel. It is comparable to a cancer in the tissue of Israel's democratic society. It's a phenomenon of an organization that takes the law into its own hands." He also warned that "Israel risked becoming an "apartheid" state if it annexed and absorbed the West Bank's Arab population". My own perception is that Rabin simply was not able to carry through on the peace he intended. I believe his assassination points in that direction.

Of course, much of the book is also about Miko's experience. He describes the difficulty of growing up the son of a general who was at one and the same time famous for his military victories and persona non grata for his outspokenness on Palestinian rights. As a child, Miko could not follow the complexity of his father's speech, although he felt the importance of it. As an adult he began having close relationships with Palestinians after his niece was killed by a suicide bomber, and he joined the Bereaved Families Forum. He found healing in sharing his grief. He also began really hearing the version of history that was different from what he had learned in school—180 degrees different.

+ + +

I Shall Not Hate by Izzeldin Abuelaish—an amazing book by an amazing man. Izzeldin Abuelaish wrote this book after three of his daughters and his niece were killed by an Israeli shell fired directly into his house, for no discernable military purpose. His nephew was shot, and almost killed, by Hamas. Dr. Abuelaish fully develops, through his own experience, the concept that the hate mongers on both sides are the same, and those who strive for peace and justice on both sides are the same.

His struggle for peace and understanding remains unshakable. On page 230, he writes: "First we must join to fight our mutual enmity, which is our ignorance of each other. We must smash and destroy the mental and physical barriers within each of us and between us. We must speak and move forward as one to achieve our brighter future; we are all living in one boat, and any harm to some people in this boat puts us all in danger of drowning. We must stop blaming each other and adopt the values of—our, us, and we."

He credits much of who he is to the dedication of his family, his teachers, and the doctors who, when he was a teenager treated him for arthritis, taking time to explain everything to him, and to seed in him an interest in the field of medicine. He also credits the kind, hospitable Israeli family that he worked for when he was fifteen, his first truly positive contact with Israelis.

Shortly after his return home from this summer job Sharon's soldiers bulldozed all the houses on his street, giving the families only a few hours to grab their possession. His family's only prized possession was a grape vine which couldn't be removed. On page sixty-two he describes his internal struggle to process this: "The paradox between the warm hospitality of the Israeli family that had employed me that summer and the brute force of Sharon's Israeli soldiers made me recognize that I had to commit myself to finding a peaceful bridge between the divides."

✦ ✦ ✦

The Waif an autobiography by Nicholas Voinov, published in January 1955. (Confusingly there seems to exist a novel by the same author, with the same title, published in 2010. I believe Nicholas Voinov is a pen name. The author refers to himself as Koyla in the book.) While the place and time of this book is Stalinist Russia, much of it describes the situation that evolves in any place in the world where there are people who do not have legal access to necessities, a subject extremely relevant to the proposals I am presenting in this Shared Land peace plan. The book is simultaneously incredibly well written and sensitive. It presents the world seen through the eyes of a child street thief, rescued from starvation, and raised by a gang. Initially the author adopted the us versus them perspective of his gang. All those who live legally are the enemy, those who caused our suffering. They show us no kindness and we show them none. This was combined with the despairing knowledge that while as a gangster, one might be powerful for a while, eventually one would be imprisoned or killed. Following, extracted from pages twenty-seven and twenty-eight, are the author's words on this subject, "After the first job (stealing) I felt the waifs are one thing and the rest of the world something different and hostile. I began to understand my waif comrades—their sullenness, bitterness, and hatred, their suspicion of everyone outside their own world. For the first time in my life, I felt a chasm separating me, as a waif, from all the people who did not live as I did. It became clear to me that the waifs were my friends, my family, and I would have to stick to them or die."

When Koyla was twelve he was exposed to another perspective. He found out that the orphanage to which he had been taken when he was eight, and in which he would have starved to death had he stayed, was now actually taking care of children. He decided to stay and try to adjust to a legal lifestyle. He went to school, learned to read and write, and loved science and art. The situation was not as clear cut as it might look. One of the reasons the children now had enough food was that one of the staff members, Uncle Fedya, sometimes took a few of the older boys to help him steal food from warehouses. Kolya saw that Uncle Fedya was an extremely skilled thief, yet he taught the boys to only steal what was needed, and to always do the least harm possible. This was a very different way of thinking.

The book is filled with Kolya's struggle to develop his own belief about right and wrong while living in a situation where confusion, dishonesty, and injustice were the norms. This is the struggle currently being experienced by many growing up in Gaza, in the West Bank, and in Israel. The reason I recommend this book is the author's unusual ability to put this struggle into words.

The Truth Shall Set Us Free and *Beyond the Two-State Solution* by Jonathan Kuttab—Kuttab is a human rights lawyer and a Palestinian. He relates his vast amount of experience in extreme detail. Together his books clearly present why the two-state solution simply cannot work, and that the problems of injustice in the Holy Land are too deep to be fixed simply by reforms. An entirely different structure is needed. He also proposes a one state solution. While his outline for this is not identical to mine, the similarities outweigh the differences.

ABOUT THE AUTHOR

I DON'T HAVE THE USUAL CREDENTIALS for writing a Middle East Peace Plan. I don't have a degree in international relations, or anything similar. What I have is a lifetime of contemplating and researching questions and realities such as—"Why would anyone kill babies? If I had been brought up by the baby killers, I too, would think it was good to kill babies."

My beloved cousin Joseph had been in a concentration camp from the age of sixteen until twenty-one. Then he had gone, for a period of time, to Israel. He saw the same nightmare starting over. This time the victims were the Palestinians. My mother was desperately clinging to the belief that Israel was the healing for the Holocaust, a shining light, and a banner of justice. I was a young person determined to understand these things, even if a took a lifetime. I looked for every cue. I contemplated why different people saw the exact same situation so differently. I realized that my mother's way of emotionally dealing with atrocities began with, "This can't be." My cousin Joseph's was the opposite. I asked him once, "When you were in the camp, were you afraid?" He said, "No. I was never afraid. Of course, I knew that at any moment I might be beaten or killed. But I wasn't afraid. It just was." This made me think that helping people to see the truth meant helping them to reduce fear, not shocking them.

I contemplated the fact that while my mother was, for a period of time, blocked by emotions from seeing the truth, her iron-clad commitment to human rights for everyone eventually got her there.

My father, who was an engineer, gave me much guidance in how to contemplate and research. "Look for the patterns. Examine the structures. To what degree do the relationships of nations reflect the relationships of individual people? Don't just look at what is wrong. Look also at what is right. We come to understandings through studying opposites. Examine what structures make communities work well, make governments work well. Contemplate what history might look like if WWI had been followed, not with the Treaty of Versailles and punishing reparations, but with support like the Marshall Plan."

All I ask of readers is to consider a future in which every side moves past the impulse to prosecute grievances and, instead, restores sanity, balance, and peace.

The website **www.balancing-power.com**

is expected to be up and running sometime

in September 2024, perhaps sooner.

This website will contain a free

downloadable PDF of the contents of this booklet,

as well as additional information.

In the meanwhile, you can send a request

for a free PDF to **balancingpower777@gmail.com.**

Questions and comments are also welcome.

I will respond to the degree that time allows.

www.ingramcontent.com/pod-product-compliance
Lightning Source LLC
Chambersburg PA
CBHW061740250726

48657CB00002B/1017